OUT CRY

"*A garden enclosed is my sister . . .*"
Song of Solomon, 4:6

By TENNESSEE WILLIAMS

OUT CRY

by TENNESSEE WILLIAMS

A NEW DIRECTIONS BOOK

Manufactured in the United States of America

Published simultaneously in Canada by McClelland & Stewart, Ltd.

First published clothbound (ISBN: 0–8112–0500–2) and as New Directions Paperbook 367 (ISBN: 0–8112–0494–4) in 1973.

New Directions Books are published for James Laughlin
by New Directions Publishing Corporation,
333 Sixth Avenue, New York 10014

DEDICATED TO THE LADY MARIA ST. JUST

OUT CRY

SKETCH OF STAGE SETTING FOR THE NEW YORK PRODUCTION BY JO MIELZINER

A DISPENSABLE FOREWORD

Having the necessary arrogance to assume that a failed production of a play is not necessarily a failed play, I have prepared this new version for publication and subsequent reappearance on other stages.

Here it is, the play, subject to your appraisal upon the printed page, under the distinguished imprimatur of my most loyal advocate in the world of letters, the publishing house of New Directions.

And as for my depression over the failed production, I think it is temporary, a nervous phenomenon responsive to the treatment of a long ocean voyage with an "outside cabin"—slowly West by way of East, a time to get it together, all of it, the memoirs, the new play, and myself.

Hopefully or *Deo volente*, as my grandfather used to say when setting out on a journey in his nineties, the cry is still *en avant*.

T.W.
1973

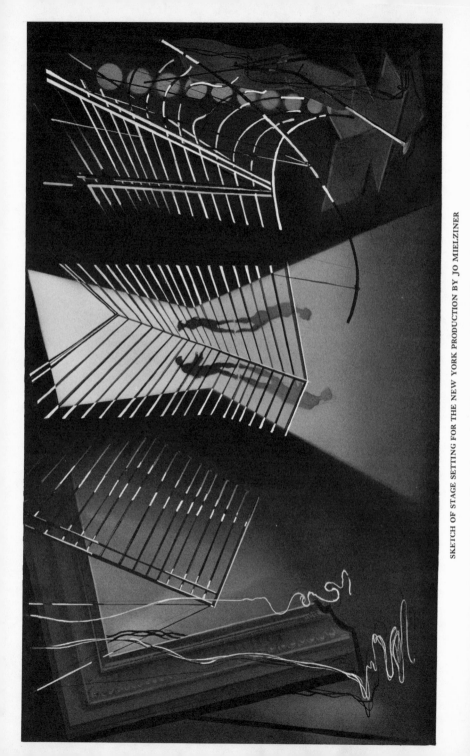

SKETCH OF STAGE SETTING FOR THE NEW YORK PRODUCTION BY JO MIELZINER

Out Cry opened at the Lyceum Theatre in New York on March 1, 1973, produced by David Merrick Arts Foundation and Kennedy Center Productions, Inc., and directed by Peter Glenville. The lighting and stage design were by Jo Mielziner, the costumes by Sandy Cole, with Alan Hall as stage manager. The cast was as follows:

FELICE   MICHAEL YORK
CLARE   CARA DUFF-MACCORMICK

An earlier version of *Out Cry* was presented in Chicago on July 8, 1971, at the Ivanhoe Theatre. It was produced and directed by George Keathley, with Donald Madden and Eileen Herlie in the principal roles. A still earlier version, under the title of *The Two-Character Play*, was offered at the Hampstead Theatre Club, London, on December 12, 1967.

SYNOPSIS OF SCENES

Before and after the performance: an evening in an unspecified locality.

During the performance: a nice afternoon in a deep Southern town called New Bethesda. Images may be projected on the stage backdrop: they should have a subjective quality, changing subtly with the mood of the play.

FELICE [*exhibiting the articles mentioned*]: Scratch pad and pencil! [*He kneels, panting, among the cushions.*] The setting isn't Morocco, the cushions just arrived without the sofa! [*He draws a deep breath to compose himself.*] Act One, Scene One. At rise of curtain I am discovered on stage alone, yes, necessarily alone since she never enters on cue and never in a condition that I can predict anymore.

CLARE [*in a strangulated cry, at a distance*]: Felice?

FELICE: I know what that cry means: she's rising reluctantly to the surface of consciousness, I—understand her—reluctance, but sometimes patience—gets impatient, you know . . . Cockroach! [*He sucks in his breath with disgust.*]—A humanizing touch! I think I read somewhere that cockroaches are immune to radiation and so are destined to be among the last organic survivors of— the great "Amen" . . .

CLARE [*same distance, a little clearer*]: Felice?

FELICE [*shouting*]: Pla-ces!—Fear . . . [*He has glanced upstage and at the "chained monster."*] Fear! —The fierce little man with the drum inside the rib-cage.—Compared to fear grown to panic that has no limit—short of consciousness blowing out and not reviving again—no other emotion a living, feeling creature is able to have, not even love or hate, is comparable in—what? —Force? —Magnitude? —Too rhetorical, that, work over later . . .—Of course you realize that I'm trying to catch you and hold you with an opening monologue that has to be extended through several— rather arbitrary—transitions, only related in a general way to— [*He gestures toward the statue with eyes shut tight.*]

CLARE [*slightly closer*]: Where!

FELICE [*flips a page of the pad without otherwise relating to it*]: —There is the love and the—substitutions, the surrogate attach-ments, doomed to brief duration, no matter how—necessary . . .— You can't, you must never catch hold of and cry out to a person,

PART ONE

Before the performance.

At curtain rise, Felice stands motionless as a hunted creature at the sound of pursuers. He is on the platform of a raked stage, a notebook hanging open from his downstage hand. There should be, at a low level, a number of mechanical sounds suggesting an inhuman quality to the (half underground) vault of a foreign theater at which he has recently arrived. He is staring from the raked platform (on which a fragmentary set has been assembled) at a huge, dark statue upstage, a work of great power and darkly subjective meaning. Something about it, its monolithic presence and its suggestion of things anguished and perverse (in his own nature?) rivet his attention, which is shocked and fearful.

Almost immediately he starts to move toward it, at first slowly and cautiously. The mechanical sounds might increase slightly in volume and tempo as he approaches the upstage edge of the platform. Then he leaps off to the pediment of the sculpture that towers over him and begins a fierce, demonic effort to push it away. It is too heavy to be moved by a man alone. He shouts for assistance.

FELICE: *Is someone, anyone, back here to help me move this—please? I can't alone!* [*There is an echo of his "alone."*] This place has an echo-only answering voice. [*A door slams off stage*] Is that you Fox? Fox! [*There is an echo of his "Fox."*] Impossible! Where did it begin, where, when? [*He runs his hands through his hair.*] This feeling of confusion began when—I can't think where. My God I've tried to conceal it, this confusion, but it's pretty obvious, now that I've shown some evidence of it . . .

[*He has taken some cushions out of an old wicker box in which "props" are carried. His speech is breathless; sometimes ironic, sometimes savage.*]

SYNOPSIS OF SCENES

Before and after the performance: an evening in an unspecified locality.

During the performance: a nice afternoon in a deep Southern town called New Bethesda. Images may be projected on the stage backdrop: they should have a subjective quality, changing subtly with the mood of the play.

Out Cry opened at the Lyceum Theatre in New York on March 1, 1973, produced by David Merrick Arts Foundation and Kennedy Center Productions, Inc., and directed by Peter Glenville. The lighting and stage design were by Jo Mielziner, the costumes by Sandy Cole, with Alan Hall as stage manager. The cast was as follows:

FELICE   MICHAEL YORK

CLARE   CARA DUFF-MACCORMICK

An earlier version of *Out Cry* was presented in Chicago on July 8, 1971, at the Ivanhoe Theatre. It was produced and directed by George Keathley, with Donald Madden and Eileen Herlie in the principal roles. A still earlier version, under the title of *The Two-Character Play*, was offered at the Hampstead Theatre Club, London, on December 12, 1967.

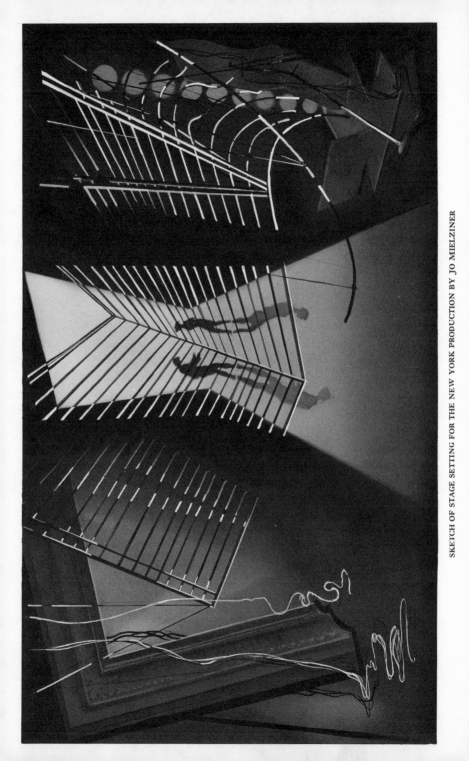

SKETCH OF STAGE SETTING FOR THE NEW YORK PRODUCTION BY JO MIELZINER

A DISPENSABLE FOREWORD

Having the necessary arrogance to assume that a failed production of a play is not necessarily a failed play, I have prepared this new version for publication and subsequent reappearance on other stages.

Here it is, the play, subject to your appraisal upon the printed page, under the distinguished imprimatur of my most loyal advocate in the world of letters, the publishing house of New Directions.

And as for my depression over the failed production, I think it is temporary, a nervous phenomenon responsive to the treatment of a long ocean voyage with an "outside cabin"—slowly West by way of East, a time to get it together, all of it, the memoirs, the new play, and myself.

Hopefully or *Deo volente*, as my grandfather used to say when setting out on a journey in his nineties, the cry is still *en avant*.

T.W.
1973

SKETCH OF STAGE SETTING FOR THE NEW YORK PRODUCTION BY JO MIELZINER

OUT CRY

DEDICATED TO THE LADY MARIA ST. JUST

loved or needed as deeply as if loved—"Take care of me, I'm frightened, don't know the next step!" The one so loved and needed would hold you in contempt of human law and resisting arrest. In the heart of this person—him-her—is a little automatic sound apparatus, and it whispers to this person: "Demand! Blackmail! Despicable! Reject it!"—And so the next morning you have to make your own coffee, your own phone calls, and go alone to the doctor to say: "I'm afraid I'm dying."

CLARE [*in the wings*]: Felice!

FELICE: Clare! [*He tosses away the scratch pad and pencil.*]

CLARE [*appearing, lighted dimly*]: Nobody called me.

FELICE: I yelled my head off.

CLARE: Oh.—Decapitated?—Sorry!—How much time have we got?

FELICE [*to the audience, rising*]: Imagine the curtain is down. [*He comes downstage and peeks through the imaginary curtain.*] They're coming in. It's nearly curtain time.

CLARE: Where is everybody?

FELICE: Everybody is somewhere, Clare. —What I have to do now is keep her from getting too panicky to give a good performance in this state theater of a state unknown, but she's not easy to fool, in spite of her—condition.

[*Clare enters, falteringly, blindly: almost at once she encounters the huge statue and utters a terrified outcry.*]

[*Felice drops an article removed from the prop basket.*]

CLARE: *Whose—monstrous aberration—is this?!*

FELICE: *I honestly don't know but it's there and it can't be moved!*

9

CLARE: It—dominates, it towers over the stage, what play on earth could be performed under this? Not even *Medea* or— *Oedipus Rex!* And— *"Can't be moved,"* did you say?

FELICE [*helplessly*]: It—won't be lighted.

CLARE: *If anything is lighted the light will catch it.*

FELICE: *Will you quit shouting with an audience out there?*

CLARE: *You* are shouting.

FELICE: Will you, please, will you—!

CLARE: Will I what?

FELICE: Your chronic hysteria's cracking my nerves, Clare, I—

CLARE: What about my nerves?—I'm also a vertebrate with a nervous system that's been subjected to shock after shock till— [*She stumbles and cries out again.*]

FELICE: CARE! —ful.

CLARE: Felice, that chained monster's *obscene!*

FELICE: I made the same observation, I tried to move it, I couldn't, I called for assistance, I got none, so now we have to forget it. And by now you surely must have noticed that on these long, long tours we run always into certain—*unalterable circumstances* that we just have to—*ignore!*

CLARE [*abruptly controlling her shock*]: Yes, I've—noticed that, too, on these long, long tours—unalterable circumstances, "Pox vobiscum," P-O-X—rhymes with Fox. . . —What I'm going to do in my leisure time from now on—while waiting for custom inspectors to, to confiscate things, and so forth, is—

FELICE: Will you please—? *Migraine!*—no codeine left! [*He is clasping his head.*]

CLARE: Is make out a list, un—unabridged—compendium of these—unexpected and—*unalterable*—*circumstance*, I'll—see you later. . .

[*She starts a slow, unsteady progress downstage, alongside the acting platform: her eyes have an unnatural, feverish brightness.*]

I forget—*unalterable circumstance*, but— Remember the time that destitute old—painter—invited us to tea on the—Viale—something—somewhere and when we arrived—the concierge said, suspiciously, "Oh, him, huh, five flights up, not worth it!"—Five flights up, not worth it! —No, not exactly worth it, the old, old painter was seated in *rigor mortis* before a totally blank canvas, teakettle boiled dry on the—burner—under a skylight—that sort of light through a dirty winter skylight is—*unalterable*—*circumstance*—but there is no skylight here, I haven't noticed a window— Is this theater under the ground? Is this the subterranean —pleasure-dome of—Kabla—Kubla—Koon?

[*During this speech, Felice has stood transfixed with dismay at her condition, motionless, an astrological chart in his hand.*]

—Sacred river must be—frozen over— [*She collides with something: a startled cry.*] *Felice!*

FELICE: Clare! —Hush!

CLARE: Will you please help me through this nightmare of debris? Why, it's like the surface of a sea where some great ship's gone under, spewing up wreckage!

FELICE: Parasol?

CLARE: Did you say "parasol"? I thought you said "parasol"—a dreadful thought. . .

FELICE: I'm checking props.

CLARE: Props, parasol—I don't want to think what I'm thinking.

11

FELICE: Strike a match and watch your step back there.

CLARE: Too late for watching my step, since I was conceived and delivered and fell into this—profession? —I will move not a step more till you remember that you are—the remnant of a gentleman *and* my brother—I will stand here motionless as that monster until you—

FELICE: Gloves!—hat. . .

CLARE: I said—

FELICE: Wait one minute, a moment. —You know, I can't tell your highs from your lows any more, Clare.

CLARE: I can't either, it's all one endless—continuum of—endurance. . .

FELICE [*cutting through*]: Bowl of soapwater but only one spool.

CLARE [*moving downstage*]: After last season's disasters we should have taken a rest on some quiet Riviera instead of touring these primitive faraway places.

FELICE: Clare, you couldn't stop any more than I could.

CLARE: I couldn't unless you stopped with me. [*She sits on the prop basket, stage left.*]

FELICE: We had to go on together. No alternative ever.

CLARE: I suppose when two people have lived together and worked together for such an—incalculably long time—it's natural to feel panicky as I felt when I recovered consciousness in that—travesty of a dressing room back there. You know what woke me up? A squeaky noise and a flapping about of wings up toward the invisible ceiling. I said to myself: "It's a bat," but I wasn't scared—I wasn't even surprised.

[*They both laugh, sadly and lightly.*]

12

That dressing room is a sight to behold, it's a filthy refrigerator, but I was so exhausted I fell right asleep in a broken-back chair.

FELICE: I'm glad you got some sleep.

CLARE: I'm still half asleep and my voice is going. Listen! My voice is practically gone!

FELICE [*still arranging props*]: Phone on piano top. —You never come on stage just before curtain time, without giving me the comforting bit of news that your voice is gone and you'll have to perform in pantomime tonight.

CLARE: It always seems to be true.

FELICE: But somehow never is.

CLARE: I try my best to understand your nervous anxieties. Why don't you try to understand mine a little?

FELICE: I do, but you have so many of them, you know. Will you come on the set, I have new business to give you.

CLARE: And *I* some to give *you*. I want you to look at me on stage, stop avoiding my eyes, I can't act with you when you won't look in my eyes like you really saw me.

FELICE: Clare, I'd continue to see you if I were stone-blind, Clare.

CLARE [*moving toward the proscenium*]: Let me have a peek at *them*.

FELICE: [*drawing her back*]: No! Don't!

CLARE: Why not?

FELICE: When you look at an audience before a performance, you play self-consciously, you don't get lost in the play.

CLARE: Why are we talking to each other like this, like tonight was the end of the world and we're blaming each other for it?

13

FELICE: You've been resting, I haven't. I'm dead-beat, I'll probably dry up several times tonight.

CLARE: You nearly always tell me your memory's gone when the curtain's about to go up.

FELICE: It always seems to be true.

CLARE: But somehow never is. [*In a frightened voice*] You have on father's astrology shirt.

FELICE [*impatiently*]: Yes, I'm already in costume.

CLARE: For *The Two-Character Play?*

FELICE: The other play is canceled.

CLARE: I have to be informed when a performance is canceled, or else I won't perform. Those stairs, those stairs aren't the stairs for *The Two-Character Play.*

FELICE: So far, only parts of the set have arrived.

CLARE: These stairs go nowhere, they stop in space.

FELICE: I have placed your gloves and parasol up there. Climb some steps and I'll say you've gone upstairs.

CLARE: Are you serious? About playing it that way?

FELICE: Desperately.

CLARE: Where is the sofa?

FELICE: It didn't arrive. We'll have to use cushions, Moroccan style.

CLARE: Are you going to throw new speeches at me tonight?

FELICE: Tonight, I feel there'll be a lot of improvisation, but if we're both lost in the play, the bits of improvisation won't matter at all, in fact they may make the play better.

CLARE: I like to know what I'm playing and especially how a play ends. *The Two-Character Play* never had an ending.

FELICE: When the curtain is up and the lights are on, you'll fly like a bird through the play, and if you dry up—use it.

CLARE: Felice, do you have a fever?

FELICE: No. Do you?

CLARE: I'm on fire with panic.

[*She starts toward the proscenium again, to peek out at the audience. He seizes her arm and drags her back.*]

You looked out. Why can't I?

FELICE: You know how bad it is for you.

CLARE: Well, just let me ask you one question. One little question only.

FELICE: All right, ask me, but don't depend on getting much of an answer.

CLARE: Can you tell me how long were we on the way here? It seemed everlasting to me. All those frontiers, I didn't know the world had so many frontiers. And God help me, Felice, I honestly don't remember where we got on the train. Do you?

FELICE: Certainly. Of course.

CLARE: Then where, tell me where?

FELICE: Oh, Clare, don't! Don't, don't question me now, save all questions till after the performance.

CLARE: Is it all right if I make a comment on your appearance?

FELICE: Yes. What?

CLARE: You have lovely hair but there's much too much of it. Why, it's almost as long as mine.

FELICE: I don't think Felice is a man who could force himself to go to a barber often.

CLARE: The part of Felice is not the only part that you play. *The Two-Character Play* is certainly the most unusual play in the repertory, but it isn't the one and only one we perform.

FELICE: From now on, it might be.

CLARE: Wouldn't *that* please the company! What would they be doing?

FELICE: I don't have any idea or a particle of interest.

CLARE: Oh! How regal! [*She pauses.*] Is this tour nearly over?

FELICE: It could end tonight if we don't give a brilliant performance.

CLARE: ALL I remember about this last trip—I must've had a fever—is that it would be light and then it would be dark and then it would be light or half light again and then dark again, and the country changed from prairies to mountains and then back to prairies again and then back to mountains, and my watch froze to death, and I tell you honestly I don't have any idea or any suspicion of where we are now except we seem to be in a huge mausoleum of a theater somewhere that seems like nowhere.

[*There is a guttural mumbling of voices from the "house." Felice pounds the stage floor again.*]

FELICE: After the performance, Clare, I'll answer any question you can think of, but I'm not going to hold up the curtain to answer a single one now.

CLARE: Felice, do you think I am not your equal?

FELICE: You're not my equal. You're my superior, Clare.

CLARE: I'm your superior in only one respect. I'm more realistic than you are, and I insist on knowing why no one is here but us two.

16

FELICE: Do you hear mumbling and growling?

CLARE: Yes, it sounds like a house full of furious unfed apes, but let's get back to my question. Where's everybody? [*She searches for a cigarette.*] Cigarette shortage.

[*She lights a cigarette with shaky fingers. Felice pounds the stage three times.*]

I said where *is* everybody? And I *insist* on an answer.

FELICE: You *insist* on an answer? You're sure you *do* want an answer?

CLARE: I do want an answer, right now.

FELICE: All right, you win, Clare, but I think you'll wish you'd lost. [*He takes a paper from his pocket.*] Here. Look at this.

CLARE: Telegram? You know I'm blind without my reading glasses. Here, strike a lucifer for me.

FELICE: Shortage of matches. [*He strikes a match and hands the telegram to her.*]

CLARE [*reading aloud, slowly*]: "Your sister and you are— *insane!*"

FELICE: Signed—"The Company." Charming?

CLARE: "We have all borrowed money to return to—" [*The match goes out. She turns to the piano and strikes a note.*] Well, as they say—

FELICE: What?

CLARE: That sort of wraps things up.

FELICE: The whole company's left us, there is no staff except for two inscrutable stagehands who came in without a word and put up this piece of the set and helped me hang the lights before they—

17

CLARE: Deserted us, too?

FELICE: I tried to make them talk but they wouldn't or couldn't. They were silent as executioners, wouldn't look at me, even, just put up the door and the curtains and then weren't there any more.

CLARE: Would you recognize them again if they came back?

FELICE: You're the one that recognizes stagehands. I smile and shake hands with them but never remember their names.

CLARE: You're always so absorbed in your work, Felice, that you hardly recognize me—I understand that, but naturally a new company wouldn't, they'd be offended by it and go into a huddle and come to the conclusion that you were a bit *dérangé*, not just an eccentric artist but *un peu dérangé*. And you'd fallen into a habit of shouting out at rehearsals, "Mad, I'm going mad!" So finally they took your word for it, Felice.

FELICE: When you read the telegram did it say that *I* was insane, me, just *me?*

CLARE: Oh, Felice, no, no, it said: "You and your sister." But Felice, you know that artists put so much into their work, that they've got very little left over for acting like other people, their behavior is bound to seem peculiar . . . even freakish. Doesn't that seem logical to you?

FELICE: The company had been with us, except for a death now and then, or a commitment to an asylum now and then, for—

CLARE: How long?

FELICE: A considerable length of time.

CLARE: A considerable length of time is not a very precise statement of exactly how much time.

FELICE [*pounding the stage floor again*]: Then *you* tell me how long!

CLARE: I've always left time up to you. [*She pauses.*] Didn't I get you a new piece of fur for the collar on that coat?

FELICE: Yes, but I preferred my mangy sable.

CLARE: Well, never mind that—what are we going to do? Something or nothing whatsoever at all?

FELICE: Only the dead can do nothing at all and get away with it, Clare.

CLARE: Yes, they do get away with it pretty nicely.

FELICE: But we're alive.

CLARE: Yes, unperished and relatively imperishable?

FELICE: The living have to do something.

CLARE: What is it going to be, in your opinion? Has anything occurred to you, or are you still waiting for a last-moment inspiration?

FELICE: We're going to do *The Two-Character Play* as we've never done it before.

CLARE: Impossible.

FELICE: Necessary.

CLARE: Some necessary things are impossible.

FELICE: And some impossible things are necessary.

CLARE: What an argument!

FELICE: No argument—decision.

CLARE: One-sided. Felice Devoto commanding, but you can't be a commander without someone to command. I won't be commanded since I know what would happen. Chaos of improvisation, new speeches thrown at me like stones, as if I'd been condemned to be stoned to death. Would you like to play with me in absolute

19

panic and in total confusion? Maybe you would, but you won't. No, thank you, Felice. This isn't the first time I've had to save you from self-destruction which would destroy me, too.

FELICE: We'll toss some new speeches back and forth at each other.

CLARE: Not I, said the fly. Felice, if we attempted to give a performance tonight, it would prove it was true.

FELICE: Prove what was true?

CLARE: What the company called us—insane. I'm going back to my dressing room and put on my coat and go to the hotel and sleep and sleep and—

FELICE: Clare, you have your coat on.

[*There is a pause. Clare strikes a chord on the piano.*]

CLARE: Do you have your brandy flask on you?

FELICE: For after the performance, not before.

CLARE: There can't be a performance.

FELICE: What is there going to be?

CLARE: An announcement by Mr. Fox that the company and the stagehands and the sets have yet to arrive here and so the performance is canceled.

FELICE [*gently and firmly*]: No. There'll be a performance of *The Two-Character Play*. [*He takes a silver flask from his pocket and offers it to her.*]

CLARE [*drinking from flask*]: Do you think—do you think they really do think we're insane, or were they just being bitchy because the long tour has been such a long disappointment?

FELICE: Since they've quit, I see no reason to think about what they think.

20

CLARE: You don't find it—disturbing? Well, I do, I find it very disturbing, because I—

FELICE: Let's discuss it after the performance.

CLARE: That witch Florence said to me on the train: "Do you and your brother always go into a trance before a performance?"

FELICE: I'm afraid you're a little confused, since that witch Florence wasn't with us this season. [*Felice goes into the wings.*]

CLARE: Even with the lights on it's cold to the bone, bone cold, and in *The Two-Character Play* we can't keep our coats on, we've got to take off our coats and make the audience and ourselves feel it's a summer day in the South.

[*She coughs. He takes off his coat, holds his hand out to take hers. She gives him her hand with a pleading look.*]

FELICE [*patiently*]: I don't want your hand. I want your coat.

CLARE: I'm not going to take off my coat in this big, filthy ice-box. If you're able to give a performance, do your pantomime for them.

[*Felice tears off Clare's coat. She cries out. He throws their coats behind the sofa; then thumps the stage again with the stick.*]

Felice, try to understand what that telegram did to me. I can't play tonight, not *The Two-Character Play*—why, I can't remember a line.

FELICE: You will when it starts, and we'll get through it somehow.

CLARE: You think you're being brave, but you're just being desperate and irrational. Felice, believe me, I'm not lying, I can't, I couldn't go through it!

FELICE: Clare, you're going to play Clare.

21

CLARE: I am going back to my dressing room, and you are going to announce the performance is canceled because of impossible circumstances.

FELICE: I am going out right now and announce the change of program, and when I come back, you will be here, on stage.

CLARE: Don't count on that. Sometimes I make decisions and stick to them.

FELICE: Feel my forehead! Sweating!

CLARE: Because you have fever.

FELICE: I'm sweating because it's a hot summer day in the South.

CLARE: —Somebody, a doctor, once told me that I had unusual courage and so did you. I said: "Oh, no, my brother and I are terrified of our shadows!" And he said: "I know that, and that's exactly why I admire your courage so much." What kind of sense does that make? Felice? I'll make the announcement in English, Spanish, and French. I'll make a lovely announcement that sometimes things just make it impossible to give a performance and I'll, I'll—I'll crouch before them with my hand held out for pity.

[*She falls to her knees. He clasps her shoulders, tenderly.*]

FELICE: The telegram was shocking, but we're both over that now. Now all we have to do is remember that if we're not artists, we're nothing. And play *The Two-Character Play* the best we've ever played it no matter what our condition of panic may be.

CLARE [*raising her hands to his head*]: Your hair's grown so long you look hermaphroditic.

FELICE: Yes? Do I? Good. Thank you. [*He thumps the stage floor with the stick and throws it behind the sofa.*]

CLARE: *Bonne chance!* I'll see you later!

[*Disregarding this threat, Felice advances to the proscenium.*]

FELICE [*to the audience*]: Good evening, ladies and gentlemen. I want you to know that my sister and I feel deeply honored to take our own small part in this enormously important idea and program of, of—cultural exchange. Of course there have been some, a number of, unexpected difficulties, but being artists of the theater we have been long prepared for working under unexpected conditions. This evening my sister and I are going to perform alone, since the rest of our company has been delayed by, uh, transportation difficulties due to the eccentricities of the weather bird, perhaps I should say the perversities of the weather bird. [*He laughs hollowly.*] However, it so happens that our favorite play in our repertory is a play for two characters, which is logically entitled *The Two-Character Play*. [*He gives the same hollow laugh, followed by a cough.*] This evening we had expected—

CLARE: Poor Felice, he's dried up. [*She puts on her coat.*]

FELICE: This play, this evening, we will now perform for you, and we hope that you will forgive the technical difficulties and problems due to the delay of our company's arrival—unavoidable—[*He bows and steps back into the setting, then speaks commandingly.*] Clare! Places! I'm going to start the play.

CLARE: You'll find me in my dressing room with the weather bird. Oh, Felice, please! *Don't* humiliate yourself!

FELICE: It's *you* that want to disgrace us! Our performance must continue. No escape!

CLARE: If you start *The Two-Character Play* it will be a one-character play, and I'll know the company's telegram is the truth.

[*Felice disappears into the wings. Clare starts blindly off the stage, then stops by the giant's statue and leans her head against its pedestal. There is the sound of curtains opening. The violet dusk of the stage that surrounds the interior set turns lighter, and strange inhuman mocking laughter is heard. At the sound of the laughter, Clare turns quickly about and defiantly faces the house. Felice returns from the wings.*]

23

FELICE: Clare! Please!

[*The mocking laughter builds. Clare throws off her coat as if accepting a challenge.*]

CLARE [*to Felice*]: Do I enter first or do you?

FELICE: Tonight you go in first.

[*Clare returns to the interior set, goes to the piano and strikes a treble note. Felice enters.*]

Your place is by the phone.

CLARE: Yes, by the phone.

FELICE: The performance commences.

[*Clare goes to the phone.*]

FELICE: Who are you calling, Clare?

[*She seems not to hear him.*]

Clare! Who are you calling?

CLARE: —Not a soul still existing in the world gone away...

FELICE: Then why are you holding the phone?

CLARE: I just picked it up to see if it's still connected.

FELICE: Is it?

CLARE: It hums in my ear. Doesn't that mean it's connected?

FELICE: The telephone company would send us a notice before they turned off the phone.

CLARE [*vaguely and sadly*]: Sometimes notices aren't—noticed.

FELICE: The house is—

CLARE: Still occupied but they might have the idea it wasn't, since it's not lighted at night and no one still comes and goes.

FELICE: We would have received a notice if one was sent.

CLARE: We can't count on that.

FELICE: We mustn't start counting things that can't be counted on, Clare.

CLARE: We must trust in things—

FELICE: Continuing as they've—

CLARE: Continued?

FELICE: Yes, as they've continued, for such a long time that they seem—

CLARE: Dependable to us.

FELICE: Permanently dependable, yes, but we were—

CLARE: Shocked when the—

FELICE: Lights refused to turn on, and it was lucky the moon was so nearly full that, with the window shades raised, it lighted the downstairs rooms.

CLARE: But we collided with things in the upstairs hall.

FELICE: Now we could find our way around in it blind.

CLARE: We can, we do. Without even touching the walls.

FELICE: It's a small house and we've lived in it always.

CLARE: You say that I was indulging in a bit of somnambulism last night.

FELICE: Clare, you had a restless night.

CLARE: You did, too.

FELICE: In a small house when—

CLARE: One of the occupants has a restless night—

FELICE: It keeps the other awake.

CLARE [*crying out*]: *Why do I have to sleep in that death chamber?*

FELICE [*controlled*]: We agreed that their room was just a room now. Everything about them's been removed.

CLARE: Except Father's voice in the walls and his eyes in the ceiling so that I can't shut mine. —That night of the accident night, you ran to the foot of the stairs but not a step further, you blocked the steps, I had to force my way past you to the room where—Mother opened the door as if I'd knocked like a visitor not—expected.

FELICE: Stop repeating, repeating!

CLARE: No sign of recognizing me at the door, no greeting, a look of surprise, very slight, till she opened her mouth on a sound-less fountain of blood, and Father behind her saw and received me quietly, too, oh, it was a quiet reception that I received at the door, quiet, polite, just a little surprised till the dreadful torrent and Father said, "Not yet, Clare," just as quietly, gently to me as *that*, before they went separate ways, she to the door of the bath-room where she fell and he to the window where he fired again looking out at—*out*. . .

[*Felice strikes his fist on piano keys.*]

And you tell me it isn't their room any more, that it belongs to me now, inherited without effort not to remember what you never entered so have no memory of?

FELICE: I said: "LET IT REST!"

CLARE: Not in that room at night? Who passed that death sentence on me?

FELICE [*with forced quiet*]: You weren't in that room last night, you came to the door of mine.

CLARE [*fearfully*]: To ask for—a—cigarette...

FELICE: We've had no cigarettes since—

CLARE: Is it improper for me not to stay in one place? All night? Alone?

FELICE: You didn't stay in one place, you wandered about the house, upstairs and down as if you were searching for something.

CLARE: Exploring the premises, yes.

FELICE: With a fine-tooth comb. —Did you find it?

CLARE: No, but I came across something, this old memento, this token of—[*She lifts her hand to show a ring.*]

FELICE: What?

CLARE: This ring with my birthstone, the opal called a fire opal.

FELICE: You haven't worn it for so long that I thought it was lost.

[*Evanescent music fades in.*]

CLARE: Mother told me that opals were unlucky.

FELICE: Frigid women are given to little fears and superstitions, and—

CLARE: Opals do have a sinister reputation. And it was a gift from Father.

FELICE: That was enough to prejudice her against it.

CLARE: Sleepless people love rummaging. I look through pockets that I know are empty. I found this ring in the pocket of an old mildewed corduroy coat which I'd forgotten I'd ever owned and didn't care if the stone was unlucky or not.

FELICE: Nothing could be unlucky that's so lovely, Clare. [*He turns it on her finger, a sort of love-making.*]

27

[*The music stops.*]

CLARE [*Striking the piano key*]: Didn't you say that you went out today?

FELICE: Yes, you saw me come in.

CLARE: I didn't see you go out.

FELICE: When you see somebody come in you know he's been out.

CLARE [*skeptically*]: How far outside did you go? Past the sunflowers, or—?

FELICE: I went out to the gate, and do you know what I noticed?

CLARE: Something that scared you back in?

FELICE: No, what I saw didn't scare me, but it, it—startled me, though. It was—

CLARE: What?

FELICE: Clare.

CLARE: What?

FELICE [*stage whisper*]: You know *The Two-Character Play.*

CLARE [*in a loud stage whisper*]: The telegram is still on the set.

FELICE: Clare, there wasn't, there isn't a telegram in *The Two-Character Play.*

CLARE: Then take it off the sofa where I can see it. When you see a thing, you can't think it doesn't exist.

[*He picks up the telegram, crumples it, throwing it out the window.*]

FELICE: There now, it never existed, it was just a moment of panic.

CLARE: What a convenient way to dispose of a panicky moment!

FELICE: Dismissed completely, like that! And now I'll tell you what I saw in the yard when I went out.

CLARE: Yes, do that! Do, please.

FELICE: I saw a sunflower out there that's grown as tall as the house.

CLARE: Felice, you know that's not so!

FELICE: Go out and see for yourself.

[*She tries to laugh.*]

Or just look outside the window, it's in the front yard, on this side.

CLARE: *Front* yard?

[*He nods but averts his face with a slight smile.*]

Now I know you're fooling.

FELICE: Oh, no, you don't or you'd go look out the window. It shot up quick as Jack's beanstalk, and it's so gold, so brilliant that it—seems to be shouting sensational things about us. Tourists will be attracted?

CLARE: Why are you—?

FELICE: Botanists, you know botanists, they'll flock to New Bethesda to marvel at this marvel, photograph it for the—*National Geographic*, this marvel of nature. This two-headed sunflower taller than a two-story house which is still inhabited by a—recluse brother and sister who never go out any more. . .

CLARE: It's such a long afternoon. . .

FELICE: It's summer, which is our season, but after the afternoon, we have to remember that there are unexpected collisions in an unlighted house, and not always only with—furniture and —walls. . .

29

CLARE: Call it the poem of two and dark as—

FELICE: Our blood?

CLARE: Yes, why don't you say it? Abnormality!— Say it! And point at me!

FELICE: At myself, first.

CLARE: Now—let's close the child's eyes and—light candles. . .

FELICE: There's no such line in the script.

CLARE [*smiling brightly*]: *Tant pire, che peccato,* meaning "too bad."

[*An abrupt change in style of performance occurs at this point, as if they were startled out of a dream.*]

FELICE: —Clare, somebody is knocking. Why don't you go to the door? Don't you hear them knocking?

CLARE: Who?

FELICE: I can't see through the door.

CLARE: I don't hear any knocking.

[*He drums the table with his knuckles.*]

Oh, yes, now I do, but—

[*He drums the table again.*]

They're very insistent, aren't they?

FELICE: Go see who's there.

CLARE: I can't imagine. I'm not properly dressed, I'm not fit to be seen.

FELICE: You're perfectly dressed and look unusually well, but me, I don't have a tie on, and this old shirt of Father's, I've sweated through it.

30

CLARE: That's excusable on a—hot afternoon. You, you let them in and say you'll call me down if it'd be they want to see *me*.

FELICE: Christ, have you reached the point where you're scared to answer the door?

CLARE: Reached and— [*She starts up the spiral stairs that stop in space.*] —The knocking's stopped. —I think they've gone away. —No! Look! They're slipping a slip of paper under the door!

[*They stare fearfully at the doorsill, the supposed piece of paper.*]

FELICE: —They've left.

CLARE: Yes, pick up the—

[*He crosses to the door and makes the gesture of picking up a card: frowns at it, breath audible.*]

FELICE: "Citizens—Relief."

CLARE: —I've never heard of such a thing in my life. Have you ever heard of Citizens Relief?

FELICE: No, I think it's wise to be cautious about things you've never—

CLARE: Heard of. It might be a trick of some kind, an excuse to—

FELICE: Intrude on our—

CLARE: Privacy, yes. Shall we destroy the card or keep it in case of a desperate situation?

FELICE: That's not a thing we seem to have to wait for, is it?

CLARE: Oh, but all the questions we'd have to—

FELICE: —Answer. . .

CLARE: Yes, there'd be interviews and questionnaires to fill out and—

FELICE: Organizations are such—

CLARE: *Cold!*

FELICE: Yes, impersonal things.

CLARE: I'll put the card under grandmother's wedding picture, just in case a desperate situation—

FELICE: Increases in desperation—

CLARE: *Anyway, here it is,* at least we—know where it is. Now I—suppose we have to prepare for—public action against us, since they know we're—still here.

FELICE: What action, such as what?

CLARE: —Removal by force of—eviction?

FELICE: You do ask for trouble by—having notions like that.

CLARE: I don't know what to do next! [*She turns about distractedly, hands clasped together.*]

FELICE: I do, I know.

CLARE: Sit there and stare at that threadbare rose in the carpet till it withers?

[*He has sunk onto the sofa, chin in hands, staring at the carpet.*]

FELICE: And you? What are you doing but clasping your hands together as if in prayer?

CLARE: Nothing unless it's something to pace about the house in a maze of amazement, upstairs, downstairs, day and night, in and out. *Out!* Oh, Felice, I want to go out, today I want to go out, I want to walk on the street—like a favorite of nature in public view without—shame . . .

FELICE: —Oh? —You want to go out calling?

CLAIRE: Yes, out calling!

FELICE: Go out!

CLAIRE: *Alone? —*Not *alone!*

FELICE: Ladies go calling alone on such nice afternoons.

CLARE: You come out calling with me.

FELICE: I can't, I have to stay here.

CLARE: For what?

FELICE: —To guard the house against—

CLARE: What?

FELICE: *Curious—trespassers!* Somebody has to stay on the premises and it has to be me, but you go out calling, Clare. You must have known when you got up this morning that the day would be different for you, not a stay-at-home day, of which there've been so many, but a day for going out calling, smiling, talking. You've washed your hair, it's yellow as corn silk, you've pinned it up nicely, you have on your dressed-up dress that you washed to go out in today, and you have the face of an angel, Clare, you match the fair weather, so carry out your impulse, go out calling. You know what you could do? Everywhere you went calling you could say, "Oh, do you know how idiotic I am? I went out without cigarettes!" And they'd offer you one at each place, and you could slip them into your purse, save them till you got home, and we could smoke them here, Clare. So! Go! [*He opens the door for her.*]

CLARE: Why have you opened the door?

FELICE: For you to go out calling.

CLARE: Oh, how thoughtful, yes, very gentlemanly of you to open the door for me to go outside without parasol or gloves, but not very imaginative of you to imagine that I'd go out alone.

33

[*They stand a moment staring at each other near the open door; her hands and lips tremble; the slight smile, mocking and tender, twists his mouth.*]

—Suppose I came home alone, and in front of the house there was a collection of people around an ambulance or police car or both? We've had that happen before. People are attracted by a sudden disturbance in a house that seemed vacant. No. I won't go out alone. [*She slams the door shut.*] My legs wouldn't hold me up, and as for smiling and talking, I think I'd have on my face the grimace of a doll and my hair would stick to the sweat on my forehead. Oh, I'd hardly sit down for this friendly call on—what friends?—before I—staggered back up, that is, if, if—the colored girl had been allowed to admit me.

FELICE: It was your idea. You shouted "Out!" not me.

CLARE: I'd never dream of going out without you in your—disturbed—*condition*.

FELICE: And *you* in *yours*.

CLARE: Me, calling, a fire engine shrieks, a revolver—bang—discharges! Would I sit there continuing with the smile and the talk? [*She is sobbing a little: her trembling hand stretches toward him.*] No, I'd spring up, run, run, and my heart would stop on the street!

FELICE [*his smile fading out*]: I never believed you'd go calling.

CLARE: Right you were about that if you thought alone—but calling? Yes, I'll do that! Phone-calling is calling! [*She rushes to the telephone and snatches up the receiver.*]

FELICE: Calling, who are you—? *Careful!*

CLARE [*into phone*]: Operator, the Reverend Mr. Wiley! Urgent, very, please hurry!

[*Felice tries to wrest the phone from her grasp: for a moment they struggle for it.*]

34

FELICE: Clare!

CLARE: Reverend Wiley, this is Clare Devoto, yes, you remember, the daughter of the—[*Then to Felice*] You have to let me go on or he'll think I'm—

FELICE: What are you! Out of your—!

CLARE [*into phone again*]: Excuse me, Reverend Wiley, there was—an interruption. My brother and I still live in our parents' home after, after the—terrible accident in the house which was reported so maliciously falsely in *The Press-Scimitar*. Father did *not* kill Mother and himself but—The house was, was—broken into by some—

FELICE: Favorite of nature?

CLARE: Housebreaker who murdered our parents, but I think *we* are suspected! Oh, it's hard to stay on here, but we do, we're still here, but such a terrible thing has been going on and on. My brother Felice and I are surrounded by so much suspicion and malice that we almost never, we hardly ever, dare to go out of the house. In the nighttime people stop and linger on the sidewalk and whisper charges, anomalous letters of obscenities are sent us, and *The Press-Scimitar*—sly allusions to us as the deranged children of a father who was a false mystic and, Reverend Wiley, our father was a man who had true psychic, mystical powers, granted only to an Aries whose element is cardinal fire. [*She is sobbing now.*] Oh, I can't tell you how horrifying it's been, why, the neighbor's child has a slingshot and bombards the house with rocks, we heard his *parents* give the slingshot to him and *tell* him to— Ha! *Another rock struck just now!*

[*She drops the phone in panic. He picks it up.*]

FELICE: Mr. Wiley, my sister has a fever.

CLARE: No.

FELICE: She's not herself today, forget what, excuse and— [*He hangs up, wipes sweat off his forehead with trembling hand.*]

35

Wonderful, that does it! Our one chance is privacy, and you babble away to a man who'll think it is his Christian duty to have us *confined* in—

[*She gasps and stumbles to the piano. She strikes a treble note repeatedly on the piano. He snatches her hand from the keyboard and slams the lid down.*]

Clare!

CLARE: You shouldn't have spoken that word! "*Confined!*" That word is not in the—

FELICE: Oh. A prohibited word. When a word can't be used, when it's prohibited, its silence increases its size. It gets larger and larger till it's so enormous that no house can hold it.

CLARE: Then say the word, over and over, you perverse monster, you—!

[*Felice turns away.*]

Scared to? Afraid of a—?

FELICE: I won't do lunatic things. I have to try to pretend there's some sanity here.

CLARE: Oh, is that what you're trying? I thought you were trying to go as far as possible without going past all limits.

[*He turns to face her, furiously. She smiles and forms the word "confined" with her lips; then she says it with a whisper. He snatches up a sofa pillow.*]

Confined, confined!

[*He thrusts the pillow over her mouth, holding her by the shoulder. She struggles as if suffocating. Suddenly she stops struggling and looks out toward the audience. She then speaks in a quiet and flat tone. Completely real.*]

Felice! There is a gunman out there. A man with a gun pointed at me.

FELICE: Clare! Please. [*Felice stares at her helplessly for a few moments, then turns to the audience and says:*] I am afraid there will have to be an interval of about ten minutes while my sister recovers. You see, she is not at all well tonight.

[*Very quietly and gently he leads her off stage. The house-lights go on.*]

AN INTERVAL OF TEN MINUTES

PART TWO

As the houselights dim Felice and Clare enter hurriedly to the side of the stage outside the set.

We see Felice forcibly drawing Clare back onto the set as the curtain rises: both are panting, and there is evidence of struggle between them during the interval. [He points to a bowl by the window.]

FELICE [*her wrist still firmly in his grip*]: What is that?—what is it doing here?

CLARE [*defiantly lifting her face to his*]: It's equipment for the amusement of children on hot summer afternoons. Have you forgotten how we blew soap bubbles on the back steps those long—

FELICE: On the back steps, yes, but don't remember that we ever blew soap bubbles here in the parlor.

CLARE: Yesterday you said, "There's nothing to do, there's nothing at all to do," kept saying it, wouldn't quit. All right. Here's soap-bubble equipment. Look! Look! I haven't forgotten how! [*She blows a bubble.*]

FELICE: —Beautiful but—they break.

CLARE: You try, it's your turn now.

[*Felice stares at her for a moment: then breaks into (desperate?) laughter.*]

What has struck you so funny?

FELICE: Madness has a funny side to it, Clare. —And we can't turn back into children in public view.

CLARE: That's my line, not yours.

FELICE [*continues to laugh the same way: then suddenly is quite sober*]: —I haven't told you something you'll have to know.

38

CLARE: You're jumping a page.

[*Felice stares at her blankly.*]

CLARE [*solicitous*]: —Have you dried up, Felice? [*She leads him to the cushions as if he were senseless: gently pushes him.*] Lean back, breathe quietly, I'll take it— From where?

[*Slight pause.*]

FELICE: When Father gave up his—

CLARE: —When father gave up his equipment, his psychic readings and astrological predictions, a few days before the *un, inexplicable*—accident!—in the house— Well, he didn't give them up, exactly.

FELICE: No, not exactly by choice.

CLARE: Mother had locked up his equipment.

FELICE: Except for this worn-out shirt of his I have on, which bears the signs of the zodiac on it, and his rising sign, and a chart of the sky as it was on the hour before daybreak of the day of his nativity here in New Bethesda!

CLARE: You know, he seemed to—accept. At least he said nothing. Not even when she spoke of State Haven to him. "Yes, I can see your mind is going again. Check yourself into State Haven for a long rest—voluntarily, or I'll—" He didn't answer these threats. He became very quiet. Except when she ordered him to cut down our sacred flowers in front of the house, and said if he didn't do it she would.

FELICE: Yes, Mother, Regina, made several threats of emasculation to—

CLARE: "You cut them down or I will." [*She continues in a different voice.*] "Do that if you dare."

FELICE: And she didn't. And he—

39

CLARE: Was restlessly quiet. Sat almost continually where you're sitting and stared at that threadbare rose in the carpet's center and it seemed to smolder, yes, that rose seemed to smolder like his eyes and yours, and when a carpet catches fire in a wooden house, the house will catch fire too. Felice, I swear that this is a house made of wood and that rose is smoldering, now! And cloth and wood are two inflammable things. Your eyes make three!

FELICE: No, four! I'm not a one-eyed Cyclops! And adding your eyes makes six!

[*She strikes a sharp note on the piano. He glares at her furiously, but she strikes the note again, louder.*]

—Line!

CLARE: Didn't you tell me you'd thought of something we have to do today?

FELICE: —Yes, it's something we can't put off any longer.

CLARE: The letter of protest to the—

FELICE: No, no, letters of protest are barely even opened, no, what we *must* do today is go out of the house.

CLARE: To some particular place, or—

FELICE: To Grossman's Market.

CLARE: There?!

FELICE: Yes, *there!*

CLARE: We tried that before and turned back.

FELICE: We didn't have a strong enough reason, and it wasn't such a favorable afternoon.

CLARE: This afternoon is—?

FELICE: Much more favorable. And I simply know that it's necessary for us to go to Grossman's Market today since—I've

40

kept this from you, but sometimes the postman still comes through the barricade of sunflowers and that he did some days ago with a notification that no more—

CLARE: —Deliveries?

FELICE: Will be delivered to the steps of—

CLARE: I knew. Payment for costlies has been long—overdue.

FELICE: So out we do have to go to Grossman's Market, directly to Mr. Grossman, and speak personally to him.

CLARE: What would we speak about to him, if we found him?

FELICE: He has an office.

CLARE: His office! Where's his office? Probably tucked away in some never-discovered corner of that shadowy labyrinth of a—

FELICE: We'll ask a clerk to tell us, to take us, to—

CLARE: If the clerk saw us, he'd pretend that he didn't.

FELICE: Not if we enter with some air of assurance and, and—importance about us, as if some unexpected, some, some—providential thing had occurred in our—

CLARE: An air of importance? To nature? And to Grossman's?

FELICE: We're going to enter Grossman's Market today like a pair of—

CLARE: Prosperous, paying customers?

FELICE: Yes, with excellent credit! We'll speak, first, to a clerk and say to him: "Please show us into the office of Mr. Grossman." We are going to go into his office, we are going to tell him convincingly that in spite of all spite and, and—contrary—accusations —Father's insurance policy will be paid to us on, say, the first of next month, yes, on September the first.

CLARE: But we know that it won't be, on the first or last day of any month of the year!

FELICE: We have to say that it *will* be!

CLARE: I don't think, I'm not so sure that—

FELICE: Don't think, don't be sure. You have a resistance to all positive actions.

CLARE: It's *I* that do the little there's still to be done here.

[*They have crossed downstage to opposite sides of the interior set: face out.*]

CLARE [*at a fast pace*]: But we've been informed by the—

FELICE [*at a fast pace*]: Acme Insurance Company.

CLARE [*at a fast pace*]: Yes, they notified us, that courtesy they did offer, and I'm sure that Grossman knows it—doesn't he know everything?—that the insurance money is—what's the word? Confiscated?

FELICE [*at a fast pace*]: Forfeited.

CLARE [*at a fast pace*]: Yes, the payment of the insurance policy is forfeited in the—what is the word?

FELICE [*at a fast pace*]: Event.

CLARE [*at a fast pace*]: Yes, in the event of a man— [*She stops, pressing her fist to her mouth.*]

FELICE [*at a fast pace*]: In the event of a man killing his wife, then himself, and—

CLARE: Forgetting his children.

FELICE: —That's what's called a legal technicality . . .

[*They turn to each other.*]

CLARE: What do you know about anything legal, Felice? I'm not impressed by your pose of—

FELICE: I know there are situations in which legal technicalities have to be, to be disregarded in the interests of human, human—

CLARE: I'm afraid you underesteem the, the huge inhumanelessness of a company called *the Acme*. Why, they wrote only three sentences to us in reply to the twelve-page appeal that we wrote and rewrote for a week.

FELICE: It was a mistake to appeal, we should have demanded.

CLARE: And you should have taken the letter to the post office instead of putting it on the mailbox for the ancient postman or for the wind to collect it.

FELICE: I put a rock on the note to the postman on the letter to the— *Will you stop driving me mad?*—*The Acme* wouldn't have answered with even three sentences if they hadn't received the twelve-page appeal—and— When terrible accidents happen, details get confused. Like you got confused the accident night? Ran downstairs and phoned a dead doctor, summoned him from a ten-year stay in Old Gray.

CLARE: Who could tell the dead from the living that night?

FELICE: But couldn't remember our address? Told his widow to send him to the house behind the sunflowers? Yes, details do get confused.

CLARE: Not when publicly published.

FELICE: Forgotten, forgotten! Publicly. Now, will you listen to me?

CLARE: Your voice is coming out of your voice box clearly.

FELICE: We must say that what we saw, there was only us to see, and what we saw was Mother with the revolver, first killing Father and then herself and—

43

CLARE: A simple lie is one thing, but the absolute opposite of the truth is another.

FELICE [*wildly*]: *What's the truth in pieces of metal exploding from the hand of a man driven mad by—!*

CLARE: What you suggest is that we confront Mr. Conrad Grossman, that favorite of nature, in this possible office of his— would there be chairs in it for us to sit down in, or would we have to stand at attention facing the, the—firing squad of his glittering, bifocaled eyes? While we stammered out this fabrication which you propose that we—

FELICE [*mockingly*]: We could look an inch over his eyes or an inch under his eyes and talk to him very fast, very, very, very—

CLARE: Together?

FELICE: Each of us would have to confirm the statements of the—

CLARE: Other.

FELICE: And keep smiling and saying "Isn't it *wonderful?*" to him.

CLARE: Isn't *what* "*wonderful*" to him?

FELICE: That, that *Acme* has at, at—last conceded that—

CLARE: Hmmm. Yes, a plan, a plot, but I think this plot, this plan is something we ought to sleep on and carry out early tomorrow, not late today.

FELICE: Today you have on the dress I call your fair-weather matching.

CLARE: Yes, repaired it and washed it in Ivory. The blouse has worn thin. Oh, I'm afraid it's . . . indecent.

FELICE: It's fetching.

CLARE: What did you call it?

FELICE: Fetching, it's very fetching.

CLARE: Fetching what? Oh, fetching new credit at Grossman's?

FELICE: And when you face Mr. Grossman, it wouldn't hurt to give him a fetching smile. Well? Well? Do we do it or forget it?

CLARE: Sometimes our fear is . . .

FELICE: Our private badge of . . .

CLARE: Courage . . .

FELICE: Right! The door is open. Are we going out?

[*Pause. She backs away from him a step.*]

CLARE: See if there are people on the street.

FELICE: Of course there are, there are always people on streets, that's what streets are made for, for people on them.

CLARE: I meant those boys. You know, those vicious boys that—

FELICE: Oh, yes. You stopped on the walk and shouted "Stop!" to the boys. Covered your ears with your hands and shouted "Stop, stop!" They stopped and they crossed the street. I said: "For God's sake, what did you think they were doing? Why did you shout 'Stop' at them?"

CLARE: You heard them, too. You were right beside me.

FELICE: I was right beside you and I heard nothing but ordinary boys' talk.

[*She rushes downstage to one side of the interior set. He goes out to the opposite side. They face out.*]

[*Lightning pace, often overlapping: the effect of a Mass recited in a church containing a time bomb about to explode.*]

45

CLARE [*overlapping*]: They were staring and grinning at me and spelling out a—

FELICE [*overlapping*]: You said they were spelling out an obscene word at you.

CLARE [*overlapping*]: Yes, an obscene word, the same obscene word that somebody scrawled on our back fence.

FELICE [*overlapping*]: Yes, you told me that too. I looked at the back fence and nothing was scrawled on it, Clare.

CLARE [*overlapping*]: If you heard nothing the last time we went out, why wouldn't you go on alone to the grocery store? Why did you run back with me to the house?

FELICE [*overlapping*]: You were panicky. I was scared what you might do.

CLARE [*overlapping*]: What did you think I might do?

FELICE [*overlapping*]: What Father and Mother did when—

CLARE [*overlapping*]: Stop here, we can't go on!

FELICE [*overlapping*]: Go on!

CLARE [*overlapping*]: Line!

FELICE [*overlapping*]: A few days ago you—

CLARE: No, you, you, not I! I can't sleep at night in a house where a revolver is hidden. Tell me where you hid it. We'll smash it, destroy it together—line!

FELICE: I took the cartridges out when I put it away.

CLARE: What good's that do when you know where the cartridges are?

FELICE: I removed them from the revolver, and put them away, where I've deliberately forgotten and won't remember.

46

CLARE: "Deliberately forgotten!" Worthless! In a dream you'll remember. Felice, there's death in the house and you know where it's waiting.

FELICE: —Do you prefer locked doors of separate buildings?

CLARE: You've been obsessed with locked doors since your stay at State Haven!

FELICE: Yes, I have the advantage of having experienced, once, the comforts, the security, the humanizing influence of—

CLARE: Locked doors!

FELICE: At State Haven!

CLARE: I'm sorry but you'd allowed yourself to lose contact with anything that seemed real.

FELICE: Seemed and real don't fit.

CLARE: Stopped speaking!

FELICE: Had nothing to speak of.

CLARE: Stared without recognition!

FELICE: With nothing to recognize!

CLARE: In a little house filled with familiar—?

FELICE: Nothing can blind you more than the familiar twisted into—

CLARE: I was here, too, and saw nothing familiar twisted into—

FELICE: Oh, I don't think you knew where you were any more, you—

CLARE: Knew enough to get out of bed in the morning instead of crouching under covers all day.

FELICE [*rushes to stairs and starts up them*]: Was that a sign of clearer—

47

CLARE: It was a sign of ability to go on with—

FELICE [*on stairs*]: Customary habits!

CLARE: An appearance of—

FELICE [*beside himself, from top of stairs*]: Fuck appearance!

CLARE: Hush! —You've hidden the revolver, give it up. I'll take it down to the cellar and smash it with the wood chopper. And then be able to sleep again in this house.

FELICE [*descending the steps to Clare; exhausted, tender*]: — People don't know, sometimes, what keeps them awake . . . [*He starts the tape. The pace slows from exhaustion.*]

CLARE: The need to search for—

FELICE: The contents of empty pockets?

CLARE: Not always empty! Sometimes there's a birthstone in them that isn't lucky!

[*Pause: they stare, panting, at each other.*

[*Very slowly, with lost eyes, he closes the door—nearly.*]

FELICE: —You have the face of an angel—I could no more ever, no matter how much you begged me, fire a revolver at you than any impossible, unimaginable thing. Not even to lead you outside a door that can't be closed completely without its locking itself till the end of—

[*She turns to face him.*]

—I haven't completely closed it, it isn't finally closed . . . Clare, don't you know that you haven't an enemy in the world except yourself?

CLARE: —To be your own enemy is to have against you the worst, the most relentless, enemy of all.

FELICE: That I don't need to be told. Clare, the door's still open.

CLARE [*with a slight, sad smile*]: Yes, a little, enough to admit the talk of—

FELICE: Are we going out, now, or giving up all but one possible thing?

CLARE: —We're—going out, now. There never really was any question about it, you know.

FELICE: Good. At last you admit it.

[*Pause*]

CLARE [*assuming a different air*]: But you're not properly dressed. For this auspicious occasion I want you to look your best. Close the door a moment.

FELICE: If it were closed, it might never open again.

CLARE: I'm just—just going upstairs to fetch your fair-weather jacket and a tie to go with it. [*She turns upstage.*] Oh, but no stairs going off!

FELICE: The set's incomplete.

CLARE: I know, I knew, you told me. I have gone upstairs and you are alone in the parlor. [*She goes up the spiral stairs.*]

FELICE: Yes, I am alone in the parlor with the front door open. —I hear voices from the street, the calls and laughter of demons. "Loonies, loonie, loonies, looo-nies!" —I—shut the door, remembering what I'd said.

CLARE: You said that it might never be opened again. [*She turns abruptly downstage.*] Oh, there you *are!*

FELICE: Yes. Of course, *waiting* for you.

CLARE: I wasn't long, was I?

FELICE: —No, but I wondered if you would actually come back down.

49

CLARE: Here I am, and here is your jacket, and here is your tie. [*She holds out empty hands.*]

FELICE: The articles are invisible.

CLARE [*with a mocking smile*]: Put on your invisible jacket and your invisible tie.

FELICE: —I go through the motions of—

CLARE: Ah, now, what a difference! Run a comb through your hair!

FELICE: —Where is—?

CLARE: The inside jacket pocket. I put it there.

FELICE: —Oh? —Yes—thanks . . . [*He makes the gesture of removing a comb from his invisible jacket.*]

CLARE: Oh, let *me* do it! [*She arranges his hair with her fingers.*]

FELICE: That's enough. That will do.

CLARE: Hold still just one moment longer.

FELICE: No, no, that's enough, Clare.

CLARE: Yes, well, now you look like a gentleman with excellent credit at every store in the town of New Bethesda!

FELICE: Hmmm . . .

CLARE: The door is shut—why did you shut the door?

FELICE: —The wind was blowing dust in.

CLARE: There is no wind at all.

FELICE: There *was*, so I—

CLARE: Shut the door. Will you be able to open it again?

FELICE: —Yes. Of course. [*He starts the tape recorder again. Then, after a hesitant moment, he draws the door open.*]

50

CLARE: —What are you waiting for?

FELICE: For you to go out.

CLARE: You go first. I'll follow.

FELICE: —How do I know you would?

CLARE: When a thing has been settled, I don't back out.

FELICE: That may be, but you are going out first.

CLARE: Will you come out right behind me or will you bolt the door on me and—

[*He seizes her hand and draws her forcibly to the door. She gasps.*]

FELICE: Out!

CLARE: See if—!

FELICE: There are no boys on the street! Stop this foolishness. Afternoons aren't everlasting you know.

CLARE: May I set my hat straight, *please*? [*She turns to a little dusty gilt-framed oval mirror to put the old straw hat on her head; it should have a touch of pathos but not be ludicrous.*]

FELICE: I thought you hated that hat.

CLARE: I certainly don't regard it as the most stylish piece of headgear in New Bethesda, but—I don't intend to make a call without a hat on my head. [*She removes the sprig of artificial cornflowers from the silk hatband and tries it in another position.*] Well, it just doesn't—

[*Felice snatches the hat off her head and tosses it on the stairs: then thrusts her through the door. She cries out a little as if dashed in cold water. He shuts the door behind them, takes her hand and leads her a few steps forward.*]

FELICE: Are you going to go on shaking like that?

51

CLARE: I will if you go on pushing me around.

FELICE: It's a—

CLARE: What?

FELICE: —Nice afternoon.

CLARE [*tensely*]: Yes!

FELICE: You couldn't ask for a nicer afternoon, if afternoons could be asked for.

CLARE: I—have no complaints about it.

[*Slight pause*]

FELICE: I don't know what we're waiting here for. Do you? [*She makes a sudden startled turn.*]

CLARE: Slingshot in the—!

FELICE: No, no, no!

CLARE: Something moved in—

FELICE: A kangaroo! Jumped!

[*Clare tries to laugh.*]

We're waiting here like it was a bus stop back of the sunflowers. And it's only a block and a half from here to Grossman's Market. So let's get a move on, slingshots, kangaroos, or—anything you can dream of. The sooner we get started the sooner we'll return with credit established again and livables and—necessities of persistence—three bags full!—including cigarettes . . .

CLARE: We mustn't—seem too greedy—all at once . . .

FELICE: Once we've assured Mr. Grossman that Acme will pay, there'll be no limit.

CLARE: You couldn't ask for a nicer afternoon, but—I think my suggestion was better.

52

FELICE: What was your suggestion?

CLARE: That *you* go to Grossman's Market and talk to Mr. Grossman.

FELICE: Alone? Without you?

CLARE: Yes, without me. I don't know why, but I'm shaking, I can't control it. It would make a bad impression on Mr. Grossman.

FELICE: You're not going to back out now. I won't allow you.

CLARE: Felice, while you're gone, I could, could, could—make a phone call to "Citizens Relief," you know, those people we wouldn't let in the house. I could tell them to come right over, and answer all their questions, and we would receive their relief even if Mr. Grossman doesn't believe the story.

FELICE: Clare, quit stalling. Let's go now.

CLARE: —I left something in the house.

FELICE: What?

CLARE: I left my—my—

FELICE: You see, you don't know what you left, so it can't be important.

CLARE: Oh, it is, it's very—it's the—cotton I put in my nose when I have a nosebleed, and I feel like I might have one almost any minute. The *lime dust!*

[*She turns quickly to the door but he blocks her, stretching his arms across the doorway. She utters a soft cry and runs around to the window. He reaches the window before she can climb in.*]

FELICE: You're not going to climb in that window!

CLARE: I am! Let me, I have to! I have a pain in my heart!

53

FELICE: Don't make me drag you by force to Grossman's Market!

CLARE: The moment I get back in I'll call the people from "Citizens Relief"!

FELICE: *Liar! Liar, and coward!*

CLARE: Oh, Felice, I—

[*She runs back to the door. He remains by the window. She enters the interior set and stares out at him, hands clasped tightly together. He steps over the low window sill, and they face each other silently for a moment.*]

FELICE: If we're not able to walk one block and a half to Grossman's Market, we're not able to live in this house or anywhere else but in two separate closed wards at State Haven. So now listen to me, Clare. Either you come back out and go through the program at Grossman's, or I will leave here and never come back here again, and you'll stay on here alone.

CLARE: You know what I'd do if I was left here alone.

FELICE: Yes, I know what she'd do, so I seize her arm and shout into her face: "Out again, the front door!" I try to drag her to it.

CLARE: I catch hold of something, cling to it! Cling to it for dear life!

FELICE: Cling to it!

CLARE: It's not on the set, the newel post of the stairs. I wrap both arms about it and he can't tear me loose.

FELICE: Stay here, stay here alone! When I go out of this house I'll never come back. I'll go and go! Away, away!

CLARE: I'll wait!

FELICE: For *what?*

CLARE: For *you!*

FELICE: That will be a long wait, a longer wait than you imagine. I'm leaving you now. *Good-bye!* [*He steps out over the low sill of the window.*]

CLARE [*calling out after him*]: Don't stay long! Hurry back!

FELICE: Hah. [*He comes forward and speaks pantingly to the audience.*] The audience is supposed to imagine that the front of the house, where I am standing now, is shielded by sunflowers, too, but that was impractical as it would cut off the view. I stand here—move not a step further. Impossible without her. No, I can't leave her alone. I feel so exposed, so cold. And behind me I feel the house. It seems to be breathing a faint, warm breath on my back. I feel it the way you feel a loved person standing close behind you. Yes, I'm already defeated. The house is so old, so faded, so warm that, yes, it seems to be breathing. It seems to be whispering to me: "You can't go away. Give up. Come in and stay." Such a *gentle* command! What do I do? Naturally, I obey. [*He turns and enters by the door.*] I come back into the house, very quietly. I don't look at my sister.

CLARE: We're ashamed to look at each other. We're ashamed of having retreated—surrendered so quickly.

FELICE: There is a pause, a silence, our eyes avoiding each other's.

CLARE: Guiltily.

FELICE: No rock hits the house. No insults and obscenities are shouted.

CLARE: The afternoon light.

FELICE: Yes, the afternoon light is unbelievably golden on—

CLARE: The furniture which is so much older than we are—

FELICE: I realize, now, that the house has turned into a prison.

CLARE: I know it's a prison, too, but it's one that isn't strange to us.

[*For the first time since he re-entered the house, they look directly at each other, slowly, with difficulty.*]

FELICE: I don't lift my arms, not willingly. —They are lifted and they extend as if they weren't a part of me. —I don't know what I feel except a sense of—danger and—longing.

CLARE: I—have no—breath.

[*She takes several faltering steps toward him: then rushes into his extended arms: there is a convulsive embrace—like two lovers meeting after a long separation. Her lips are whispering against his face—inaudible words.*]

FELICE: Not—possible, the—stairs don't go upstairs, the steps—stop in—space!

CLARE: There's nothing, then, but—

[*Very gently, he thrusts her away from him: her eyes turn away from him too.*]

FELICE: "A garden enclosed is my sister . . .

CLARE: What did I do with the card from Citizens Relief?

FELICE: You put it under—

CLARE: Oh. Grandmother's wedding picture. [*She lifts the picture and looks at it yearningly for a moment.*] A coronet of pearls, a hand lifting the veil from her radiant face.

FELICE: Clare, we've seen that picture all our lives. It's the card under the picture you picked the picture up for.

CLARE: To get the office number.

FELICE: Of Citizens Relief. It might close early you know.

CLARE: I'm going to call them at once.

FELICE: Make it just a simple dignified appeal for—necessary—assistance.

CLARE: Simple, dignified, yes.

[*She has crossed to the phone but her hand stops short of the receiver. He picks it up and thrusts it into her hand. She lifts it to her ear.*]

It makes no sound. I feel like screaming "Help, help!"

FELICE: —Is it—?

CLARE [*hanging up the receiver*]: Sometimes a phone will go dead temporarily, just for a little while, and come back to life, you know.

FELICE: Yes, I know. Of course.

CLARE: —So we stay here and wait till it's connected again?

FELICE: We might have to wait till after the Relief Office closes. It might be a better idea to ask the people next door if we can use their phone since something's gone wrong with ours.

CLARE: That's right. Why don't you do that?

FELICE: *You* do that. It's the sort of thing you could do better. Look! [*He points at window.*] The woman next door is taking some clothes off her washline. Call her through the window.

[*Clare catches her breath. Then rushes to the window and calls out in a stifled voice:*]

CLARE: Please, may I, please, may we—!

FELICE: Not loud enough, call louder.

CLARE [*turning from the window*]: —Did you really imagine that I could call and beg for "Citizens Relief" in front of those malicious people next door, on their phone, in their presence? Why, they gave their son a slingshot to stone the house! When-

57

ever they catch a glimpe of us through a window, they grin like death.

[*Slight pause.*]

FELICE: You asked me what people did when they had nothing at all left to do.

CLARE: I asked you no such thing. [*After a moment, she dips a spool in the soapy water.*]

FELICE: Instead of calling the woman next door through the parlor window, you blow soap bubbles through it. Did you blow the soap bubbles out the window as an appeal to the world? They are lovely as your birthstone. They rise through the fading afternoon light. But they are a sign of surrender, and we know it. —And now I touch her hand lightly, which is a signal that I am about to speak a new line in *The Two-Character Play*. [*He touches her hand.*] Clare, didn't you tell me that yesterday or last night or today you found, you came across, a box of cartridges for Father's revolver?

CLARE: No! No, I—

FELICE: Clare, you say "yes," not "no." And then I pick up the property of the play which she's always hated and dreaded, so much that she refuses to remember that it exists in the play.

CLARE: I've said it's—*unnecessary*.

[*Felice has picked up a revolver from under the sheet music on the piano top.*]

Has it *always* been there?

FELICE: The revolver and the box of cartridges that you found last night have never been anywhere else, not in any performance of the play. Now I remove the blank cartridges and insert the real ones as calmly as if I were removing dead flowers from a vase and putting in fresh ones. Yes, as calmly as—

58

[*But his fingers are shaking so that the revolver falls to the floor. Clare gasps, then laughs breathlessly.*]

Stop it!

[*Clare covers her mouth with her hands.*]

Now I—[*He pauses.*]

CLARE: Have you forgotten what you do next? Too bad. I don't remember.

FELICE: I haven't forgotten what I do next. I put the revolver in the center of the little table across which we had discussed the attitude of nature toward its creatures that are regarded as *unnatural* creatures, and then I— [*After placing the revolver on the table, he pauses.*]

CLARE: What do you do next?

FELICE: Yes, I put on the tape and then I—I pick up my spool and dip it in the water and blow a soap bubble out the parlor window without the slightest concern about what neighbors may think. Of course, sometimes the soap bubble bursts before it rises, but this time please imagine you see it rising through gold light, above the gold sunflower heads. Now I turn to my sister who has the face of an angel and say to her: "Look! Do you see?" [*He mimes the action of blowing soap bubbles.*]

CLARE: Yes, I do, it's lovely and you made it . . . and it still hasn't broken.

FELICE: Sometimes we do still see the same things at the same time.

CLARE: Yes, and we would till locked in separate buildings and marched out at different hours, you by bullet-eyed guards and me by bullet-eyed matrons. [*She strikes a note on the piano.*] Oh, what a long, long, way we've traveled together, too long, now, for separation. Yes, all the way back to sunflowers and soap bubbles, and there's no turning back on the road even if the road's backward, and backward.

[*The tape machine misses and plays the music at triple tempo, which rises to a sound like a kind of shriek.*

[*Clare removes her white cotton gloves, glances at her brother's tranced face: he stares past her blindly. She draws a breath: then crosses to the machine and stops its playing.*

[*A couple of beats: silence.*]

—Well, that's that. [*She crosses to pick up her cloak.*] Put on your coat, Felice, I'm putting on mine, and I'll remove this— bewitching bit of millinery from my corn-silk head now. [*She takes off her hat, fiercely snatching the sprig of cornflowers from its band and tossing it to the floor.*]

FELICE [*blankly*]: What?

CLARE: Felice, come out of the play! The house is completely empty.

FELICE: Walked? Out? All?

CLARE: Yes, yes, were you unconscious? One stood up down front with a grunt and the others all followed suit and shuffled out—en masse! And I'm glad the torture is over!

FELICE: *It—wasn't—your play!*

[*She brings him his coat.*]

CLARE: No, but you *wrote* it for me. Have I expressed my appreciation enough? [*She throws his coat about him and tries to button it.*]

FELICE: Don't! —Don't put things on me I can put on myself! This is not State Haven!

CLARE: —Only three smokables left. Soooo!—they've broken our rice bowl. —Smoke?

60

[*She hands him a cigarette. He looks out blindly.*]

Here! —And now call Fox. See if there's cash enough to get us out of this place to somewhere further south of the—Arctic Circle.

[*There is a pause. Felice is afraid to call Fox, who may be gone.*]

Well, for God's sake, call him!

FELICE [*calling into the house*]: Fox! —*Fox!*

CLARE: Faithful Fox is silent as the proverbial—

FELICE: *Fox!*

CLARE: *Fox, Fox, Fox!*

TOGETHER: *Fox!*

[*There is an echo from their call.*]

CLARE: I'll tell you an unpleasant thought that's entered my head. Fox has absconded with the box-office receipts.

FELICE: Well, we'll track him down.

CLARE: I don't feel like fox hunting.

FELICE: Then what do you feel like?

CLARE [*lying down on the cushions*]: Like falling into bed at the nearest hotel and sleeping the next thousand years.

FELICE: Well, go get your things.

CLARE: Get what things?

FELICE: Your purse, your handbag for instance.

CLARE: I don't have one to get.

FELICE: You've lost it again?

CLARE: I told you days ago that my bag had disappeared and it hasn't returned. What have you got in your wallet?

61

FELICE: Phone numbers and addresses of people mostly forgotten.

CLARE: Did we start with no money or just arrive here with no money?

FELICE: Things have kept disappearing. Isn't that how it was?

CLARE: Don't ask me how anything was, or is, or will be.

FELICE: When you make remarks of that kind, other people take them literally.

CLARE: This still seems like a performance of *The Two-Character Play*. The worst thing that's disappeared in our lives—I'll tell you what it is. Not the company, not Fox, not brandy in your flask, not successes that give confidence to go on—no, none of that. The worst thing that's disappeared in our lives is being aware of what's going on in our lives. We don't dare talk about, it's like a secret that we're conspiring to keep from each other, even though each of us knows that the other one knows it. [*She strikes a piano key.*] Felice, about the play. *The Two-Character Play.* I wonder sometimes if it isn't a little too personal, too special, for most audiences. Maybe—

FELICE: What do you mean by "too special"?

CLARE: Too personal, that's all, such as using our own names in it, and—

FELICE: At the first reading of it, you made a hypocritical remark. You said: "Why, it's like new wine, it has to be properly aged, so don't let's include it in this season's repertory."

CLARE: I said no such thing but I can tell you who did. It was poor old Gwendolyn Forbes that said that, and that's not all she said. She also said *The Two-Character Play* is a tour de force, it's more like an exercise in performance by two star performers, than like a play, a real play.

FELICE: There was never anyone by that name—what name did you say?—in the company.

CLARE: Felice, there was hardly a soul in the company whose name you could remember. The person I'm talking about is the one that burned to death in that hotel fire in—wherever it was— in some place—

FELICE: Oh. Her. She had a passion for incineration. Burned to death in a hotel fire and then had herself cremated.

CLARE: People burned to death don't have themselves cremated. We're both too tired to make sense. Call a limousine to pick us up and take us to a hotel.

[*Felice sits on the piano stool.*]

Felice, you're as tired as I am. Help me get up. My legs are gone.

[*He rises to help her but topples onto the cushions.*]

Thank you. Will we ever get up. We're sitting here panting for breath like a couple of dogs. Last cigarette, unless you have some.

FELICE: No. [*He lights her cigarette.*]

CLARE: We'll share it. Felice, is it possible that *The Two-Character Play* never had an ending? [*She passes the cigarette to him.*]

FELICE: Even if we were what the company called us in the telegram, we'd never attempt to perform a play that had no end to it, Clare.

CLARE: Then tell me how it ends, because I honestly can't remember a bit of it past the point where we stopped tonight.

FELICE: *The Two-Character Play* doesn't have a conventional ending.

CLARE: I don't mind that, that's fine, but what's the unconventional ending? Or can't you remember any better than I can?

[*He hands her the cigarette.*]

It never seems to end but just to stop, and it always seems to stop just short of something of a disturbing nature when you say: "The performance is over."

FELICE: It's possible for a play to have no ending in the usual sense of an ending, in order to make a point about nothing really ending.

CLARE: I didn't know you believed in the everlasting.

FELICE: That's not what I meant at all.

CLARE: I don't think you know what you meant. Things do end, they do actually have to.

FELICE: Well— [*Rising*] Up! Hotel! Grand entrance! We'll face everything tomorrow.

CLARE: Just before the performance you told me that Fox the foxy hasn't made us hotel reservations here, wherever here is!

FELICE: The one hotel in town is directly across the street from the theater, and we'll enter in such grand style that we'll need no reservations.

[*He crosses hurriedly into the wings and she starts to follow, but her exhaustion stops her at the upstage edge of the platform, facing the statue.*]

CLARE [*to the statue*]: —Unalterable—circumstance—unaltered. . .

[*Offstage, frantic sounds begin to be heard, running footsteps, fists pounding and feet kicking at metal: muffled cries faintly echoed. This should continue at a varying pitch during Clare's solitary presence on the stage and should sometimes catch her attention.*

[*She slowly turns about to face downstage in a spot of light.*]

Well, he lost his argument about the impossible being necessary tonight. I think the impossible and the necessary pass each other on streets without recognition, could sit side by side without sign of the slightest aquaintance before or now or—ever. . .

[*Metallic crash, off stage.*]

Felice! —Well, it wasn't always all lost. —There were nights of— triumph, ovations—times of public honor! Memorable—celebrations— Crossing the Tiber in an open carriage, over that bridge of stone angels, when, suddenly, a hailstorm stung our faces and hands with little flowers of ice that made us sing and sing! [*She sings a snatch of "Come le rose" or "Dicitencello Vuoie." Stops, hearing distant shouts.*] Felice? —Oh, and that night in the wine garden on the Danube, the lights of a river boat, Russian soldiers singing in chorus! [*She sings a verse of the Russian Gypsy song "Coachman, don't whip the horses, I have no where to hurry to, I have no one to love"—(words in Russian). More pounding and shouting, muted.*] Felice! —"Your sister and you—insane, and so—" "Do you always go into a trance before a performance?" —"Yes, and after one, too." —Long dead now, many—gone. . . Felice, Felice!—when he finds that I am not following him as I've done all my life, he won't be coming back here with glad tidings, or a corsage of violets to pin on my—

[*She touches the lapel of her coat as Felice returns. He seems not to see her at first: he's breathless and stunned.*]

Well? —Have we met with some *new*—unalterable circumstance now?

[*He collapses among the cushions.*]

—Yes, I can see there's been another disaster. Let's put the props back into the old prop basket while we—prepare. . . [*She gathers up all but one cushion on which he has fallen and throws them into the battered wicker basket.*] Aren't you going to speak to me? Ever? Again?

FELICE: Clare, I'm afraid we may have to stay here a while.

CLARE: In this frozen country?

FELICE: I meant here in the theater.

CLARE: Oh!

FELICE: Yes, you see the front and back doors are locked from the outside, and as you know this building is windowless as a casket.

CLARE: Does this mean we have to stay here freezing till they open the building in the morning?

FELICE: Clare, there's no guarantee they'll open up the building in the morning or even in the evening or any morning or even after that.

CLARE: Out! Out! Out! [*Crazed with panic, she whirls about and snatches up the "play" phone. She realizes what it is and drops it as if it had scorched her hand.*]

FELICE: Hysteria won't help, Clare.

CLARE: The, the backstage phone?

FELICE: Disconnected as the phone in the play was.

CLARE: I think that this is some sort of dramatic metaphor that you are trying to catch me in, but I refuse to be caught!

FELICE: Even if it were possible to, would I want to?

CLARE: Obviously you accept this, it was your play and this is the end you want!

FELICE: Clare, I want no end but—

CLARE: —But?

FELICE: There seems to be no choice but—

CLARE: To march between the chaplain and warden conducting us to the execution chamber without resistance?

FELICE: The sentence was passed such a long time ago that the dread of execution is worn out. Fear *does* have a limit. Contrary to my—opening—monologue, even fear has a limit. . .

CLARE [*tonelessly*]: Monologue? —Opening?

FELICE [*with a passion of something—self-derision? despair?— but with a passion*]: *I'd started a new play. —I would have been too tired to finish it, though.*

CLARE [*again abstracted*]: —Oh . . .

FELICE [*with the same bitter force*]: Just this evening, before you entered, I composed the opening monologue of a play that's —closed! Unopened. . . [*He throws his head back in a (silent?) self-mocking laugh—make sure it's not self-pity.*] You could put it *this* way. Fear is limited by the ability of a person to care any more.

CLARE: For anything but—

[*She clasps his head against her. A hollow metallic sound is heard.*]

I hear.

FELICE: This empty vault is full of echoes and echoes and echoes. The heat has been turned off and metal contracts with cold.

CLARE: That's a lovely elegiac note in your voice! Are you paralyzed there? Yes, you, but not me, I am not paralyzed, I am going to find the way out. [*She makes aborted moves in several directions, terrified of the dark that surrounds the dimming area of the stage: at each rush stops short with sharply arrested gestures.*] *Human Out Cry!*

67

FELICE: Give it up, Clare, give it up, it's useless. There are punctuation marks in life and it's time to admit that they include periods—one of which is final. . .

CLARE: Who do you think you're addressing? You're talking to your insanely practical sister, not to violet-haired Drama Club Ladies, digesting—*vol-au-vent* and *pêche-Melba.*—Felice, please! It's cold. It's not like the cold anywhere on the planet Earth, it's like the cold at the far, the further, the go-no-more last edge of space. . . So it's a prison, this last theater of yours.

FELICE: Yes, it would seem to be one.

CLARE: I've always suspected that theaters are prisons for players. . .

[*The sound of distant explosions*]

Listen! Gunfire! Bombardment!

FELICE: Or holiday firecrackers blocks away. . .

[*The sound of distant gunfire.*]

Clare, you're not frightened, are you?

CLARE: I'm too tired to be frightened, at least not yet. That's strange, you know, because I've always had such a dread of being locked up, caught, confined in a place—it's the greatest dread of my life. No, what I feel right now is bone-tired and bone-cold. Otherwise I'd get up and see for myself if these awful mysteries you've reported to me are exactly as you've reported.

FELICE: Do you think I've just imagined them, dreamed them, Clare?

[*He goes out the door of the interior set. Clare becomes panicky.*]

CLARE: Felice! Where are you going?

68

FELICE: To get the telegram from the company. [*He returns with it and smoothes it out on the table. He looks at it as if he had just received it.*]

CLARE: You have a dark thought in your head and I think I know what it is.

FELICE: Sometimes we have the same thoughts at the same time.

CLARE: It's getting colder and colder, moment by moment.

FELICE: During the performance—

CLARE: Yes, such as it was or wasn't—

FELICE: It was cold even with the lights on us, but I was so lost in the play that it seemed warm as summer.

CLARE: You're suggesting that—

FELICE: We must go back into the play.

CLARE: But with the stage so dim—

FELICE: If we can imagine summer, we can imagine more light.

CLARE: When we're lost in the play.

FELICE: Yes, completely lost in *The Two-Character Play.*

CLARE: We could try it, we could give it a try.

FELICE: Other alternatives lacking.

CLARE: Could we keep on our coats?

FELICE: Oh, we could, I suppose, but I think the feeling of summer with sunflowers and soap bubbles would come more easily to us if we took our coats off.

CLARE: All right. Do we stop where we stopped tonight or do we look for the ending?

FELICE: Don't worry about the ending, it'll come to us, Clare. I think you'll find it wherever you hid it.

CLARE: Wherever *you* hid it, not me. [*She catches her breath, suddenly, and raises a hand to her mouth.*]

FELICE: Is something wrong?

CLARE: No!—no—

[*He helps her remove her coat. As he removes his, she hugs her shoulders against the cold. He takes the revolver off the table.*]

FELICE: The properties of the play are the properties of our lives. Where would you like me to hide it?

CLARE: Under a sofa pillow?

FELICE: Yes, I guess that will do.

[*He places the revolver under the pillow. Clare starts the tape.*]

CLARE: And we'll find the end of the play?

FELICE: By the time we come to the end, we'll be so lost in the play that—

CLARE: The end will simply happen.

FELICE: Yes, just happen.

CLARE: Where shall we start, at the top of the play, the phone bit?

FELICE: Yes, take your place by the phone. The performance commences.

CLARE: When a performance works out inevitably, it works out well. [*She lifts the telephone.*]

FELICE: Who are you calling, Clare?

CLARE: Not a soul existing in the world gone away.

FELICE [*very fast*]: Then why did you pick up the phone?

CLARE: To see if it's still connected.

FELICE: We would have been notified if—

CLARE: It's a mistake to depend on—notification. Especially when a house looks vacant at night. [*She hangs up the phone.*]

FELICE: Night, what a restless night.

CLARE: Wasn't it, though?

FELICE: I didn't sleep at all well and neither did you. I heard you wandering about the house as if you were looking for something.

CLARE: Yes, I was and I found it. [*She pauses.*] Are you lost in the play?

FELICE: Yes, it's a warm August day.

CLARE [*raising a hand, tenderly, to his head*]: I'm sure Acme and Mr. Grossman will believe our story. We can believe it ourselves, and then livables, and necessities of persistence will be delivered through the barricade of—

FELICE: Go straight to the tall sunflowers.

CLARE: Quick as that?

FELICE: That quick!

CLARE: Felice, look out the window. There's a giant sunflower out there that's grown as tall as the house.

[*He draws a long breath, then leans out the window.*]

FELICE: *Oh, yes, I see it. Its color's so brilliant that it seems to be shouting!*

CLARE: Keep your eyes on it a minute, it's a sight to be seen.

[*She crosses to the sofa: lifts the pillow beneath which the revolver is concealed: gasps and drops the pillow back: looks toward Felice.*]

FELICE: Hurry, it won't hold!

71

[*She crosses to him and touches his hand.*]

CLARE: —Magic is a habit.

[*They look slowly up at the sunflower projections.*]

FELICE: —Magic is the habit of our existence. . .

[*The lights fade, and they accept its fading, as a death, somehow transcended.*]

CURTAIN

Please Do Not Remove Card From Pocket

YOUR LIBRARY CARD
may be used at all library agencies. You
are, of course, responsible for all materials
checked out on it. As a courtesy to others
please return materials promptly — before
overdue penalties are imposed.

The SAINT PAUL PUBLIC LIBRARY

DEMCO